The Cheat Code to
Connection Before Compliance

Leadership Strategies for Engagement-Centered Accountability Systems

Jonas Royster & Armand King

Hood Proverbz, LLC and Ariginal One, LLC
The Cheat Code: Connection Before Compliance
Leadership Strategies for Engagement-Centered
Accountability Systems

For permissions contact:
info@hoodproverbz.com
Jonas Royster
30450 Haun Road #1041
Menifee, CA 92584
jonasroyster@hoodproverbz.com
www.hoodproverbz.com

Printed Worldwide
First Printing 2026
First Edition 2026
ISBN: 979-8-9887279-7-2

Co-Published by Hood Proverbz and Walk With Me Impact Media & Education in association with Paradise Publishing Company

Table of Contents

Introduction

The Shift: From Monitoring to Engagement-Centered Leadership

We did not enter this work as policy analysts. We entered it as individuals who once sat across from authority trying to understand whether we were being seen as people or defined by our worst decisions. We remember meetings where adults spoke about us rather than with us. We remember agreeing to plans we did not fully understand, aware of the consequences but unclear on the purpose.

We also remember how differently things shifted when someone explained the "why" before enforcing the "what." That perspective stayed with us.

Years later, working alongside probation departments, child welfare teams, educators, behavioral health professionals, and community providers, we began to see a consistent pattern: most structured systems are designed around accountability, but few are intentionally designed around engagement. And that difference shapes outcomes.

Evolving Expectations

Across jurisdictions, particularly in California through initiatives like CPIP, expectations have evolved. Engagement is now measurable. Collaboration is visible. Data integrity matters. Meeting effectiveness matters. Youth and family voice matter. Cross-system alignment matters.

Accountability still matters. Structure still matters. Public safety still matters. But monitoring alone is no longer sufficient.

Systems are increasingly evaluated not only on whether expectations are enforced, but on whether participation, alignment, and follow-through are strengthened. Policy can mandate meetings, but it cannot mandate engagement. Policy can require assessments, but it cannot generate honesty. Policy can define consequences, but it cannot create ownership. Interaction determines those outcomes.

The Argument for Sequencing

This book does not argue against accountability. It argues for sequencing it strategically. Connection before compliance is not softness; it is **disciplined leadership**. When engagement precedes enforcement, accountability stabilizes. When correction precedes clarity, defensiveness increases.

Communication is not a personality trait. It is an intervention. And leaders determine whether it is treated that way.

The chapters ahead outline a practical framework for designing accountability systems that build ownership, reduce reactive cycles, and strengthen measurable stabilization.

Structure without engagement produces short-term order. Structure with engagement produces lasting stability. Stability is the true measure of leadership.

Chapter 1

Communication as Intervention: Why Engagement Determines the Quality of Accountability

Every accountability-based system has structure. Court mandates. Case plans. Behavioral expectations. Service requirements. Documentation standards. Structure is necessary. It protects safety. It creates clarity. It establishes boundaries.

But structure alone does not determine outcomes. Communication does.

Communication is the delivery system for every expectation, consequence, plan, and correction. It determines whether a rule feels arbitrary or purposeful. Whether a meeting feels collaborative or evaluative. Whether a caregiver feels partnered or blamed. Whether an assessment produces honesty or guarded responses.

The Difference Between Compliance and Ownership

There is a critical distinction leaders must understand. Compliance is external. Ownership is internal. Compliance can be observed in the room. Ownership reveals itself when no one is watching.

Compliance can be produced through authority alone. Ownership requires connection, clarity, and inclusion. When individuals comply only because supervision is present, behavior often shifts once oversight decreases. When individuals understand expectations, feel included in planning, and see how accountability connects to their development, accountability becomes internalized rather than imposed.

Modern leadership requires designing systems that produce ownership — not simply observable adherence.

Engagement Is Not Abstract

Engagement is measurable. It shows up in observable ways:

- Who speaks in meetings.
- Whether youth and caregivers influence planning.

- Whether strengths are identified alongside needs.
- Whether action steps are realistic.
- Whether follow-through happens between touchpoints.

When participation narrows, information narrows. When information narrows, planning weakens. When planning weakens, escalation cycles increase. These are not personal failures. They are **engagement breakdowns**. And engagement breakdowns are usually communication breakdowns.

Leaders who ignore communication quality often experience higher strain — more repeated violations, more reactive meetings, more documentation, more burnout. Leaders who treat communication as structural experience something different: earlier barrier identification, clearer planning, and fewer reactive cycles.

Communication Shapes Culture

Culture is not created by policy statements. It is created by repeated language. How staff describe individuals internally. How supervisors frame case discussions. How leadership talks about violations. How partners are referenced in meetings. How expectations are introduced and reinforced.

Language becomes culture. Culture becomes behavior. Behavior becomes outcome.

If internal discussions focus only on what was not done without exploring why, field interactions will mirror that posture. If leadership models curiosity before correction, officers will replicate it. If leadership tolerates identity-based labeling, that language will embed itself in documentation and court narratives.

You cannot build engagement externally if engagement is not modeled internally.

Communication Under Stress

Accountability systems operate under pressure. Heavy caseloads. Court timelines. Crisis response. Staffing shortages. Family instability. Under stress, professionals revert to habit.

Without intentional reinforcement, communication defaults to directive phrasing, immediate correction, minimal exploration, and efficiency over dialogue.

Efficiency matters. But ineffective communication creates more work long-term. More repeated violations. More escalations. More rework across agencies. More staff fatigue.

Treating communication as a personality trait limits development. Treating it as a **professional competency** elevates performance. It can be trained. It can be reinforced. It can be evaluated. It can be standardized. When communication is engineered rather than assumed, accountability becomes more precise, and precision reduces escalation.

The Leadership Decision

Every Chief, Director, and Supervisor faces a choice: Is communication an assumed skill — or an intentional intervention strategy?

If it is assumed, variability becomes the norm. Variability produces inconsistency. Inconsistency weakens engagement. If it is engineered, engagement becomes predictable. Predictable engagement stabilizes accountability.

Modern accountability systems are no longer evaluated solely on enforcement metrics. They are evaluated on engagement quality. Communication is the lever that moves that metric.

The next chapter introduces the structured framework for designing engagement intentionally — so that connection precedes correction, and accountability produces ownership rather than defensiveness.

Because structure without engagement produces short-term order. Structure with engagement produces long-term stability. And stability is the true measure of leadership.

Chapter 2

The Engagement Framework: Designing Accountability Systems That Produce Ownership

Engagement is not accidental. It is designed.

In structured systems, accountability is carefully engineered. Conditions are defined. Consequences are outlined. Timelines are monitored. Documentation is required. Engagement, however, is often assumed.

When engagement is assumed rather than structured, supervision defaults to correction-first interactions. Correction-first systems tend to produce defensiveness. Defensiveness narrows participation. Narrowed participation weakens planning. Weak planning increases escalation.

The Framework Interrupts That Pattern

The Engagement Framework is built on three operational principles:

- **Transparency**
- **Authenticity**
- **Accountable Challenge**

In sequence, these principles create the conditions under which accountability produces ownership rather than surface compliance.

Transparency: Clarity Before Enforcement

Transparency is the deliberate removal of ambiguity. In many accountability systems, individuals understand the rule but not the rationale. They know what is required but not how it connects to growth. They understand the consequence but not the purpose.

When purpose is unclear, compliance becomes transactional. Transparency shifts that dynamic. Strategic transparency means:

- Explaining why expectations exist.
- Clarifying the function of assessments and meetings.
- Naming the intended outcome of conditions.

- Making the logic of consequences explicit.

Transparency does not dilute authority. It strengthens it. When expectations are explained clearly, defensiveness decreases. When individuals understand the "why," participation increases. When participation increases, planning precision improves.

Clarity builds psychological safety. Safety increases engagement. Engagement strengthens accountability.

Authenticity: Alignment Between Message and Presence

Authenticity is consistency between what is said and how it is delivered. In structured systems, professionalism is necessary. Boundaries matter. Authority must be clear. But emotional detachment is often misinterpreted as indifference.

Authenticity does not require oversharing. It requires alignment. Alignment between words and tone. Between expectations and follow-through. Between accountability and respect.

Individuals — especially youth and families navigating high-stress systems — are highly attuned to inconsistency. If tone feels performative or scripted, trust narrows. If enforcement feels personal rather than structured, resistance increases.

Authenticity stabilizes interactions. When individuals believe the person enforcing expectations is consistent and grounded, corrective conversations become more productive. Authenticity protects credibility. And credibility is the foundation of influence.

Accountable Challenge: Correction Through Relationship

Connection without accountability produces drift. Accountability without connection produces adversarial dynamics. Accountable Challenge integrates both. It is the disciplined sequencing of correction through relationship rather than reaction.

In practice, this means:

- Clarifying the behavior without labeling identity.
- Inviting explanation before escalating consequences.

- Reaffirming expectations clearly.
- Aligning consequences with development, not frustration.
- Adjusting plans when barriers are identified.

This is not permissiveness. It is precision. When individuals feel heard before being challenged, their capacity for reflection increases. Reflection increases the likelihood that consequences produce learning rather than resentment.

Correction delivered through frustration escalates. Correction delivered through structure stabilizes. Leaders who model regulated accountability create cultures where challenge is expected — but not feared.

Sequencing Matters

The order of operations determines outcome. If supervision begins with challenge, defensiveness increases. If supervision begins with transparency and authenticity, challenge becomes productive. This is the central principle of Connection Before Compliance.

It is not about removing consequences. It is about sequencing them in a way that increases ownership. Ownership is built when individuals understand expectations, feel included in planning, recognize the logic of consequences, and experience accountability as structured rather than personal.

When ownership grows, supervision intensity often decreases. Not because standards were lowered — but because capacity increased.

Leadership Embedding

Frameworks do not shift culture unless they are reinforced. Chiefs, Directors, and Supervisors embed the Engagement Framework by:

- Modeling sequencing during case reviews.
- Evaluating engagement quality, not only outcome metrics.
- Reinforcing barrier analysis before escalation.
- Monitoring documentation tone for identity labeling.
- Coaching staff on regulated corrective dialogue.

Culture does not change through policy memos. It changes through repeated modeling. When leadership consistently sequences transparency, authenticity, and accountable challenge, that pattern becomes the default posture of the organization. And when it becomes the default, engagement is no longer dependent on personality. It becomes structural.

The Engagement Framework is not a motivational concept. It is an **operational architecture**.

In the next chapter, we move from interpersonal framework to system implementation — examining how engagement is operationalized within structured accountability environments.

Chapter 3

Operationalizing Engagement in Structured Systems: What Accountability Systems Are Actually Measuring

Structured systems often believe they are measuring compliance. Increasingly, they are measuring engagement.

Across jurisdictions and disciplines, fidelity tools now evaluate meeting effectiveness, data accuracy, cross-system alignment, participant voice, and follow-through between touchpoints.

Whether called CPIP, quality improvement review, fidelity audit, or performance evaluation, the underlying question is consistent: *Are individuals meaningfully engaged in structured accountability — or simply present within it?* That distinction determines long-term outcomes.

Procedural Compliance vs Relational Fidelity

Most systems are capable of procedural compliance. Meetings can be scheduled. Assessments can be completed. Documentation can be submitted. Participants can be invited.

But procedural completion does not guarantee relational fidelity. Relational fidelity exists when individuals understand their role in the plan, their voice influences decisions, strengths are identified alongside needs, action steps are clear and realistic, and follow-through is reinforced consistently.

When relational fidelity is absent, accountability becomes mechanical. Mechanical accountability increases surface adherence but often fails to produce ownership. And without ownership, escalation cycles tend to repeat. This is not a system failure of effort. It is a system failure of **engagement architecture**.

Dialogue as Data Integrity

In structured systems, assessments shape planning. Whether using formal tools like CANS or internal evaluation instruments, the quality of data depends on the quality of dialogue.

When conversations are rushed, defensive, or transactional, responses narrow. When responses narrow, data narrows. When data narrows, planning weakens. Weak planning increases reactive cycles.

Data accuracy is not only a technical function. It is relational. If individuals do not understand why questions are being asked, honesty decreases. If caregivers feel blamed, disclosure narrows. If strengths are not explored intentionally, planning skews toward deficit framing.

Leadership must recognize: engagement quality directly influences data integrity. And data integrity drives system credibility.

Meeting Architecture Matters

Structured systems rely heavily on meetings — case conferences, team reviews, planning sessions. Meeting quality is often assumed. It should be engineered.

Momentum-building meetings share common elements:

- Participants are prepared beforehand.
- Purpose is clarified at the outset.
- Strengths are identified before needs are addressed.
- Roles are clearly articulated.
- Action steps are assigned precisely.
- Follow-through expectations are defined.

Procedural meetings lack that architecture. They may satisfy scheduling requirements but fail to generate alignment. When alignment fails, participants receive mixed messaging. Mixed messaging increases confusion. Confusion increases instability. Stability requires coherence. Coherence is built through structured facilitation.

Alignment Across Systems

Structured accountability rarely exists in isolation. Probation interacts with child welfare. Schools interact with families. Behavioral health providers coordinate with case managers. Community organizations support court-involved youth.

When messaging differs across systems, individuals absorb that fragmentation. One professional emphasizes accountability. Another emphasizes healing. Another emphasizes compliance timelines. Without alignment, the individual at the center navigates competing expectations.

Alignment does not require identical mandates. It requires integrated messaging. Leadership should ensure role boundaries are clear, legal parameters are explained transparently, shared goals are articulated explicitly, and disagreements are resolved before final messaging is delivered.

Alignment reduces rework. Misalignment multiplies it.

From Enforcement Model to Stabilization Model

Modern structured systems are shifting. The question is no longer only *Did the rule get enforced?* The question is *Did enforcement increase stability?*

Stability includes decision-making capacity, family alignment, clear understanding of expectations, consistent cross-system messaging, and reduced reactive cycles.

Enforcement without engagement may produce short-term order. Engagement-centered accountability produces longer-term stabilization. This is not philosophical. It is operational.

Leadership Leverage Points

Leaders operationalize engagement by:

- Reinforcing preparation before formal meetings.
- Evaluating engagement quality alongside outcome metrics.
- Encouraging barrier analysis before escalation.
- Monitoring documentation tone.
- Integrating cross-system communication standards.
- Treating communication as part of performance evaluation.

When engagement is embedded into operational standards, it becomes predictable rather than personality-dependent. Predictability increases stability.

CPIP as Culture Signal

In California, the County Practice and Improvement Plan (CPIP) has formalized what many departments have sensed for years: engagement quality is now part of the measurement framework. CPIP is not simply asking whether meetings occur or assessments are completed. It is evaluating whether youth voice influences planning, whether cross-system collaboration is visible, whether strengths are meaningfully integrated, and whether accountability contributes to measurable stabilization.

Departments that treat CPIP as a documentation requirement risk narrowing its impact. Departments that treat CPIP as a cultural shift — one that aligns communication, facilitation, and supervision sequencing — position themselves to lead rather than react.

Structured systems will always require accountability. The question is whether accountability is delivered through mechanical enforcement — or through engagement-centered architecture.

Chapter 4

Engagement Under Stress: Preventing Withdrawal from Becoming Escalation

We once worked with a young person who rarely spoke in meetings. His caregiver would arrive frustrated, defensive, and visibly exhausted. In early sessions, the room would tighten quickly — correction would begin, voices would elevate, and the youth would withdraw further. Nothing technically inappropriate was happening. Expectations were clear. Consequences were outlined.

But engagement was narrowing. It wasn't a discipline problem. It was a stress response cycle.

Structured systems are high-pressure environments. Youth navigating accountability are often managing fear, uncertainty, peer influence, identity development, and public labeling. Caregivers may be balancing employment instability, transportation barriers, housing stress, and their own unresolved trauma.

Recognizing Developmental Withdrawal

Under stress, participation narrows. Narrowed participation is often misinterpreted as defiance. It is more frequently a protective response. Leadership determines whether that response triggers escalation — or invites recalibration.

Youth who are not engaging yet may offer minimal responses, avoid eye contact, miss appointments intermittently, dismiss goals, or blame external circumstances. Caregivers under strain may express frustration sharply, miss meetings, shift blame toward the system, or appear inconsistent in follow-through.

If these behaviors are framed internally as attitude problems, correction intensifies. If they are framed as **diagnostic signals**, supervision becomes precise. The distinction matters.

The Escalation Loop

When narrowed participation meets immediate correction, a predictable cycle forms. Withdrawal increases. Authority tightens. Participation narrows further. Consequences escalate. Trust decreases.

This loop can feel justified in the moment. It is rarely stabilizing over time. Breaking the loop requires sequencing.

Curiosity Before Correction

Curiosity does not replace accountability. It precedes it. Instead of beginning with escalation:

- Clarify what occurred.
- Invite explanation.
- Reflect understanding.
- Reaffirm expectations.
- Adjust structure if barriers are legitimate.

This sequence preserves authority while reducing defensiveness. When individuals feel heard before being challenged, cognitive processing improves. When cognitive processing improves, accountability becomes instructional rather than adversarial.

Correction delivered through frustration escalates. Correction delivered through structure stabilizes.

Assessing Caregiver Capacity

Structured systems often assume caregiver capacity without assessing it. Some caregivers are managing work schedules that conflict with meeting times, limited transportation access, housing instability, childcare demands, and their own mental health challenges.

When capacity is assumed rather than evaluated, plans fail. Capacity assessment is not excuse-making. It is **structural precision**. When caregivers feel seen rather than judged, collaboration strengthens. When collaboration strengthens, follow-through improves.

Engagement as a Shared Responsibility

Engagement under stress is not solely the responsibility of youth or caregivers. It is a shared system responsibility. Leaders must reinforce internally: withdrawal is information. Frustration is often fear expressed outwardly. Narrow participation signals misalignment. Escalation should follow barrier exploration, not precede it.

When this posture becomes cultural, escalation rates often decrease. Not because standards were lowered. Because structure became more precise.

Supervisor Coaching Levers

Supervisors should regularly ask:

- Was explanation invited before consequence?
- Were barriers explored?
- Was tone regulated?
- Did the individual articulate understanding of expectations?
- Does the plan reflect realistic capacity?

If participation consistently narrows after interactions, engagement quality not merely behavior should be examined. Engagement breakdowns rarely correct themselves. They compound.

Preventing Mechanical Accountability

Mechanical accountability enforces conditions. Engagement-centered accountability builds capacity. The difference is visible over time.

In mechanical systems, compliance may occur in the room but fade outside it. In engagement-centered systems, individuals can articulate why expectations exist, what skills they are building, what barriers they face, and how they will adjust next time. That articulation signals ownership. Ownership reduces the likelihood of repeated escalation cycles.

Under stress, accountability systems tend to tighten. Leadership determines whether they also become more intentional.

Chapter 5

Cross-System Leadership: Preventing Fragmentation in Structured Accountability Systems

In one cross-system meeting, a youth sat quietly while three professionals spoke in sequence. Probation emphasized curfew adherence and court compliance. A therapist emphasized emotional regulation and trauma triggers. A school representative emphasized attendance requirements.

Each professional was correct. But the messaging was not integrated. The youth left with three separate priorities, no clear sequencing, and rising anxiety about how to satisfy all of them simultaneously.

Nothing in that meeting violated policy. But stability did not increase. This is how misalignment compounds.

Parallel Mandates, Shared Outcomes

Structured systems operate under different mandates. Probation may focus on court conditions and public safety. Child welfare may focus on placement stability and permanency. Behavioral health providers may focus on therapeutic pacing. Schools may focus on academic performance and attendance.

These mandates are not competing values. They are parallel responsibilities. Fragmentation occurs when messaging is delivered independently rather than integrated. Youth experience the fragmentation first.

Conflicting instructions increase confusion. Confusion increases stress. Stress increases instability. Alignment reduces that friction.

Unified Messaging

Unified messaging does not require identical priorities. It requires coordinated framing.

Instead of "You must follow curfew" and separately "You need to manage emotional triggers," a coordinated message might sound like: "Managing emotional triggers will make it easier to meet curfew expectations. These goals support one another." That integration reduces perceived conflict.

Leadership must encourage pre-meeting coordination among professionals, clarification of role boundaries, agreement on messaging before delivery, and resolution of disagreements privately rather than in front of youth and caregivers. When alignment is visible, trust increases.

Narrative Drift and Reputation

Every department develops a reputation among partner agencies. Probation may be perceived as rigid. Providers may be perceived as overly lenient. Schools may be perceived as inflexible.

Unchecked narratives shape behavior. If probation internally describes providers as "slow," collaboration weakens. If providers frame probation as "only enforcement," engagement narrows.

Leadership must monitor internal language about partners. Language discipline protects cross-system trust. Trust improves coordination. Coordination reduces rework.

Conflict as a Leadership Function

Disagreement across systems is inevitable. The issue is not disagreement itself; it is where and how it occurs.

Effective cross-system leadership ensures that disagreement remains focused on youth outcomes, is expressed professionally, is resolved before final plans are communicated, and does not position youth in the middle of professional tension.

When youth observe professionals debating in adversarial tones, engagement narrows. When youth observe coordinated problem-solving, stability increases. Leadership modeling sets that standard.

Information Flow and Precision

Structured systems rely on information sharing. When information is unclear, delayed, or inconsistently explained, planning precision weakens.

Leaders should reinforce clear explanations of what information is shared and why, respect for confidentiality boundaries, accurate documentation that reflects collaborative input, and defined ownership of action steps across agencies.

Precision reduces duplication. Duplication increases frustration.

Cross-System Alignment as Strategy

When engagement-centered communication is embedded across agencies, systems experience fewer conflicting directives, clearer action-step ownership, stronger follow-through, reduced escalation cycles, and improved credibility with courts and stakeholders. Because alignment reduces strain. Misalignment multiplies it.

Cross-system collaboration is not secondary work. It is leadership work. Connection before compliance applies beyond individual supervision. It applies to how agencies interact with one another. Respect first. Clarity second. Accountability third. Shared structure fourth.

Because alignment reduces strain. Misalignment multiplies it.

Chapter 6

Language as Cultural Architecture: How Everyday Phrasing Shapes Identity, Planning, and System Credibility

Language does more than describe behavior. It defines identity.

In structured accountability systems, certain phrases become normalized: “Noncompliant.” “Uncooperative.” “Refuses services.” “Defiant.” “Poor decision-maker.” These terms may feel efficient in a busy staffing meeting. But efficiency is not neutral.

Language shapes perception. Perception shapes intervention. Intervention shapes outcome. Leadership determines whether language builds capacity or hardens labels.

How Language Quietly Shapes Culture

Consider a routine internal case review. A youth’s missed appointments are discussed. One staff member says, “He’s just noncompliant. We’ve talked about this multiple times.” The conversation moves quickly. The label settles in the room. The discussion shifts toward consequences.

An alternative framing might sound like: “He’s not engaging with the current expectation yet. What barrier are we missing?”

The difference is subtle. But it changes everything. The first framing defines identity. The second invites analysis. The first narrows solution pathways. The second expands them.

Internal language becomes external posture. If a youth is repeatedly described through deficit shorthand in staff meetings, that posture will surface in documentation, court reports, and supervision tone. Culture is not declared. It is repeated.

From Compliance Framing to Capacity Framing

Compliance-focused language asks: Did the rule get followed? Was the condition met? Was the expectation satisfied?

Capacity-focused language asks: What skill is still developing? What barrier needs adjustment? What strength can be leveraged? What support alignment is missing?

Compliance measures behavior. Capacity builds stability. Both matter. But long-term engagement depends on capacity development. When identity-based labels dominate, planning becomes reactive. When behavior-based descriptions dominate, planning becomes strategic.

Documentation and Court Credibility

Documentation tone influences more than internal morale. It shapes judicial interpretation, cross-agency perception, placement decisions, and future supervision posture.

A report that reads "Youth continues to demonstrate noncompliance and poor choices" communicates frustration. A report that reads "Youth continues developing decision-making skills under peer influence and would benefit from structured accountability with reinforced support alignment" communicates strategy.

The second version does not minimize seriousness. It signals thoughtful supervision. Courts value insight. Growth-oriented documentation strengthens institutional credibility.

Identity vs Behavior

Leadership must enforce a clear distinction: describe behavior, do not define identity.

"Youth missed two sessions" is behavior. "Youth is irresponsible" is identity. Identity-based labeling narrows perceived potential. Behavior-based description preserves the possibility of growth.

When individuals repeatedly hear identity-based language, internal narratives form around those labels. When they hear capacity-based language, growth remains visible.

Language and Staff Identity

Language also shapes professional identity. If staff culture revolves around catching violations, officers begin to experience themselves primarily as enforcers. If staff culture emphasizes capacity-building within structured accountability, officers experience themselves as developmental leaders.

That shift influences morale. Morale influences retention. Retention influences system stability. Language is not cosmetic. It is **cultural infrastructure**.

Leadership Enforcement of Language Standards

Chiefs and Supervisors must treat language as a measurable competency. This includes challenging deficit shorthand during staffing, reviewing documentation tone for identity labeling, modeling growth-oriented phrasing, reinforcing barrier analysis before escalation, and ensuring strengths are named explicitly.

Before finalizing documentation or recommendations, staff should ask:

- Does this describe behavior or define identity?
- Does this open a solution pathway?
- Does it preserve dignity while maintaining accountability?
- Does it reflect the individual's voice?

If the answer is no, refine it. Language repetition creates culture. Culture repetition creates system identity.

The Strategic Impact

Departments that intentionally shift language culture often experience reduced adversarial interactions, stronger cross-system collaboration, improved engagement in meetings, more accurate assessment dialogue, greater credibility in court, and increased staff alignment.

Because perception shapes intervention. Intervention shapes behavior. Behavior shapes outcomes.

Connection before compliance begins long before a corrective conversation. It begins in how individuals are described when they are not in the room.

Chapter 7

Institutionalizing Engagement: Coaching, Modeling, and Sustaining Growth Over Time

Culture does not change because a framework is introduced. It changes because behavior is modeled, reinforced, and repeated.

In high-pressure accountability systems, regression is natural. Caseloads increase. Timelines compress. Crises emerge. Under stress, professionals revert to habit. If engagement-centered communication is not reinforced intentionally, correction-first patterns quietly return.

Institutionalizing engagement is not about adding more rules. It is about strengthening coaching.

Leadership as Modeling

Staff mirror what leadership models. If supervisors open case reviews with curiosity, officers replicate curiosity in the field. If leaders regulate tone during conflict, that regulation becomes normalized. If chiefs speak about youth in growth-oriented language, that posture filters downward.

If leadership tolerates labeling, escalation-first language, or reactive tone, those patterns embed themselves into supervision culture.

Modeling is not symbolic. It is instructional. Every staffing conversation is a training moment. Every documentation review is a cultural reinforcement point. Every cross-system meeting is a signal about what the department values. You cannot delegate engagement. You must demonstrate it.

Coaching Over Correction

Institutionalizing engagement requires moving from performance management alone to developmental coaching. Supervisors should regularly ask:

- What barrier analysis occurred before escalation?
- How was purpose explained?

- What sequencing was used before corrective action?
- Did the individual articulate understanding of expectations?
- What strengths were identified alongside concerns?

These questions do more than evaluate compliance. They evaluate engagement quality. When officers are coached on sequencing, tone, and framing, not only outcome metrics, but engagement becomes repeatable.

Coaching reinforces growth in staff the same way supervision reinforces growth in youth.

Between-Meeting Reinforcement

Engagement is not sustained through formal meetings alone. Between structured touchpoints, ownership must be reinforced. This does not require lengthy sessions. It requires consistent reflective dialogue.

Questions such as: *What decision felt hardest this week? What barrier showed up? What adjustment would help next time? What strength did you rely on?*

Build reflective capacity. Reflective capacity strengthens decision-making. Decision-making capacity reduces repeated escalation cycles. When reflection is embedded into supervision rhythm, accountability becomes developmental rather than episodic.

Preventing Cultural Regression

All systems regress under pressure unless reinforcement is intentional. Warning signs of regression include increased identity-based labeling in staff meetings, escalation recommendations without documented barrier analysis, reduced youth participation in meetings, caregiver withdrawal, and documentation that reflects frustration rather than strategy.

Leaders should periodically audit meeting tone, documentation framing, engagement sequencing, and cross-system collaboration patterns. Not to discipline. But to recalibrate.

Culture shifts slowly and reverts quietly. Reinforcement prevents drift.

Growth Over Time

Institutionalizing engagement is not a short-term initiative. It is an identity shift.

When staff begin to see themselves not only as monitors of conditions but as developers of capacity, supervision changes. When youth can articulate what they are learning — not just what they must do — accountability deepens. When caregivers feel partnered rather than judged, alignment strengthens. When cross-system professionals describe one another respectfully, collaboration stabilizes.

Growth in individuals requires growth in institutions. Institutions grow when leaders model, coach, and reinforce deliberately.

The Leadership Commitment

Engagement-centered systems do not eliminate accountability. They deliver it through structure, clarity, and regulated presence.

Coaching builds staff capacity. Staff capacity builds youth capacity. Youth capacity reduces system strain. Institutionalizing engagement is not about softening standards. It is about strengthening them through development rather than reaction.

In the final chapter, we step back and ask a larger question: What does it look like when accountability systems move beyond supervision and into restoration?

Chapter 8

From Supervision to Restoration: Moving Beyond Completion Toward Lasting Stability

The goal of structured accountability has never been permanent oversight. It has been stabilization. And ultimately, graduation.

Many individuals complete supervision. Fewer graduate from it. Completion means requirements were satisfied. Graduation means capacity was strengthened. Completion closes a case. Graduation changes a trajectory.

The distinction matters. When supervision ends without ownership, the system pauses risk rather than reducing it. When supervision ends with strengthened decision-making, aligned support, and internalized accountability, the likelihood of re-involvement decreases.

Modern leadership must decide which outcome defines success.

What Restoration Means in Structured Systems

Restoration is not a legal designation. It is a leadership outcome. In structured accountability systems, restoration means:

- Individuals understand why expectations existed.
- They can articulate the skills they developed.
- Caregivers feel included rather than sidelined.
- Plans were co-developed rather than imposed.
- Cross-system messaging was coherent rather than fragmented.
- Accountability was delivered with clarity and dignity.

Restoration does not remove consequences. It ensures consequences produce growth. It shifts supervision from surveillance to stabilization. It moves the system from reaction to intention.

The Leadership Imprint

Every Chief, Director, and Supervisor leaves a cultural imprint. That imprint determines how staff talk about individuals internally, how meetings are facilitated, how violations are framed, how partners describe collaboration, and how accountability feels to those under it.

Leadership is not only about policy enforcement. It is about tone, modeling, and sequencing. It is about whether correction comes first or clarity does. It is about whether individuals leave supervision feeling managed or strengthened.

A Final Leadership Reflection

Before closing this book, consider:

- When individuals leave your system, can they explain what they learned?
- Can they articulate the skills they strengthened?
- Do caregivers describe partnership rather than blame?
- Do cross-system partners experience alignment rather than friction?
- Does documentation reflect strategy rather than frustration?
- Do staff see themselves as monitors of behavior or developers of capacity?
- Would an external observer see connection before correction?

If the answers are moving toward yes, your culture is evolving. If not yet, the opportunity remains.

The Sequence

Structured systems will always require accountability. The question is how that accountability is delivered. Mechanical enforcement produces short-term order. Structured engagement produces long-term stability.

Connection before compliance is not a slogan. It is a sequence. When transparency precedes enforcement, when authenticity stabilizes interaction, when challenge is delivered through relationship, when language preserves dignity, when alignment replaces fragmentation, when coaching reinforces growth, supervision becomes more than oversight.

It becomes development. It becomes stabilization. It becomes restoration.

And leaders who understand that sequence will define the future of accountability systems.

Outro

Continuing the Work

If this book resonated, the work does not end here.

Structured accountability systems across California and beyond are navigating increasing expectations — CPIP fidelity, cross-system collaboration, engagement metrics, documentation precision, and measurable stabilization outcomes. Shifting culture requires more than agreement. It requires reinforcement.

What We Offer

We partner with departments and agencies seeking to:

- Strengthen CPIP readiness through engagement-centered leadership.
- Improve CFT facilitation and youth voice integration.
- Increase CANS dialogue accuracy and documentation precision.
- Reduce reactive violation cycles.
- Coach supervisors in sequencing transparency, authenticity, and accountable challenge.
- Align probation, child welfare, and service partners around unified messaging.
- Shift from compliance-focused language to capacity-focused supervision.

Our work includes executive leadership briefings, department-wide engagement intensives, supervisor coaching cohorts, cross-system alignment workshops, and CPIP culture strategy sessions.

The Invitation

Connection before compliance is not a slogan. It is a sequence. If your department is ready to operationalize that sequence intentionally, we welcome the conversation.

Armand L. King
info@lawrichconsulting.com
info@wwmimpact.com

Jonas U. Royster
jonasroyster@hoodproverbz.com
info@hoodproverbz.com

Made in the USA
Las Vegas, NV
22 May 2026

47431480R00020